Well-Come Grace

**A poetic memoir of resilience
through faith and in therapy**

Suzanne Tocher

Highland
hb

First published as two works:

1) Well Connected in 2001 by Philip Garside Publishing, New Zealand and 2) Well-Come Grace in 2010, self-published by the author.

This combined and revised edition published in 2013 by Highland Books Limited, 2 High Pines, Knoll Road, Godlaming, Surrey, GU7 2EP

ISBN-13: 978-1897913-90-1
ISBN-10: 1-897913-90-7

Well-Come Grace

Contents

Part Two: Second Bite at the Olive

Beloved Olive Tree

Epilogue

Dedicated to my father — and all men
who have suffered
trauma from war,
and to my mother – a determined,
compassionate, loving
and graceful spirit.

Foreword

Well-Come Grace highlights the journey those with Body Dysmorphia have frequently travelled. A traumatic journey for most of being misdiagnosed and misunderstood over an illness identified decades ago, which until recently was considered a rare occurrence. Today we know Body Dysmorphia is a common disorder and that those who suffer eagerly await the asking of the question "are there parts of your body you feel are ugly?". For those who answer "yes" their suffering is readily apparent. Daily torment is the norm and recovery sought for their illness that remains invisible to most.

Well-Come Grace is inspirational to those with Body Dysmorphia who wish to climb out of the grips of their illness to lead a more fulfilling life.

Professor Don Jefferys
Adjunct Professor
School of Psychology Deakin University
Burwood Vic Australia

Author's Note

Body Dysmorphia is a preoccupation with a defect in appearance. The defect is either imagined or exaggerated and causes significant distress and impairment of normal social functioning.

My therapy process began at the age of twenty-two in the year 1978, after being in a mental hospital the previous year. Although there was one major break from this process between the years 1989 to 1996 when I spent time setting up my life (career, marriage, birth of my daughter), I did not complete therapy until August 2005 at the age of forty-nine. Throughout this whole journey I worked with the same therapist.

Part One was originally written during my therapeutic process before my therapist and myself in conjunction with the revealing power of God's grace, had unravelled Body Dysmorphic Disorder (BDD). In my early therapy journey, few people including professionals had even heard of BDD. In fact it was not until the first edition of *The Broken Mirror* which was published in 1996, that word started to get out about this under-recognized but yet devastating illness (K. A. Phillips, 2005).

Part Two revisits my early years and breakdowns with the insight that BDD had been underlying all the trauma and mental illness of my formative years.

Born in 1955 in Hastings, New Zealand, I grew up in a family with three siblings, two sisters and one brother. Between Parts One and Two, there are poems of appreciation for my family.

Where am I now? The book ends with an allegory where I compare my progress to that of a gnarled but resistant olive tree; Christian churchgoers will remember that Paul uses this same metaphor applying it to God's true people. Throughout the book I have placed olive images to symbolise healing. These are contrasted to images of barbed wire signifying war and imprisonment.

My mother came from a large, loving, Irish Australian family. My grandfather served in World War I and fought in the Battle of Lone Pine at Gallipoli. On returning home wounded he became an alcoholic.

My father was brought up by Scottish parents who came to New Zealand in the early 1900s. His father worked as a community constable. It was a harsh life. In the middle years of World War II, after leaving Boarding School, my father became an officer at the Featherston-based Japanese Prisoner-of-War Camp. From there he served overseas in Egypt and Italy. The war, combined with his background, caused him overwhelming trauma and loss. His only way to cope was to control. Our family took on the structure of the military as he re-enacted his trauma. .

PART ONE:

The First Bite At The Olive

Whoever drinks of the water that I shall give him shall never thirst; the water that I shall give him shall become in him a well of water springing up to eternal life.

John 4:14

Marching Orders

The General takes me
into the detention quarters,
shutting the door behind him.
He quickly walks over to the window
and rips the curtains shut.
His lips are tightly pressed together
into a long thin line.
He comes to me,
grabs and throws me
down to my bed.
Then he raises his hand and strikes
again and again
and again and again...
At last he stops,
moves away from the bed
and out of the door,
shutting it tightly.

I stand alone in a swirl
of mist and darkness.
There is a kindergarten building
just behind me but it seems vague
and distant.
The General has dropped me off early
to fit in with his tight work schedule.

Light is beginning
to come through the darkness now
and I hear a rooster crowing
cock-a-doodle-do,
cock-a-doodle-do,
cock-a-doodle-do.
For a long time I wait
for the kindergarten teacher to arrive.

Switching in,
switching out.
Real feelings hidden,
locked away.

Art Commentary

Here is a collage of various drawings and jottings;
putting them into a single jigsaw puzzle helped
me make sense of them. The small child at centre
represents me in my early years; bricked in, no way
out, thus being unable to process true feelings. Each
drawing symbolises the split I would operate out of
instead. You could think of these splits as my false self;

Switching in, switching out.
Real feelings hidden
locked away.

this false self is made up of a set of splits which are a defence designed (sub-consciously) to protect my true self by hiding it.

The jottings tell the thoughts I had in each split and whenever I operated from a particular split, my thoughts and behaviours were always the same.

The switch and lit-up bulb on top left show that when I'm in one split, I am disconnected from all other splits. Since the jotting is small, I will summarise the splits for you starting at the top left: 1/ The puppet who relies on affirmation from others to feel in control. 2/ The flight reflex "I want to go home." 3/ Mirror on the wall, am I okay? 4/ Vigilance, the cost of safety. 5/ Obedience to the general. 6/ Dyslexia undermines me. 7/ Rebelling against 'The General'.

These splits will re-occur in further illustrations. You can see them online at greater magnification (link at www.highlandbks.com under the book catalogue entry, valid for 2013/4).

INTO MY TEENS

We move camp. The General has a job in a country school and he is going to be the headmaster. He is feeling very proud and powerful for he now has two battlefields under his command — our camp and the school.

He settles well into these war zones and feels there are many changes to be made in both areas. He has closely surveyed the land to the back of the school house and notices wild cats playing in the long grass and trees. The General is not impressed with the lack of discipline.

In due course a shiny brown rifle appears in our camp. The General positions himself on the porch of his fortress and fires at the cats as he sees them.

The trees in the back area also begin to bother the General, so he organises a bulldozer. No negotiation with the parents of the school. Resistance from the staff, resistance from the parents.

The General has a breakdown and we move camp again.

Each day starts with my barracks light snapped on. The General is on his 5:45am morning round. My bed covers are ripped back. Not a minute is to be wasted. The troops must now gear into action for the day. There's a tight schedule ahead and no deviation from this is acceptable.

I roll over and the despair of the day hits me. I haul myself out of bed and go to the ablution block. Back in the barracks, the sound of the General's electric shaver filters through the wall. The timing is precise as usual. This is my cue to dive back into bed, pull the blankets back up around my neck, shut my eyes and with one ear cocked ready to hear the shaver being turned off, grab a few minutes more rest.

Suddenly the shaver snaps off and I jolt out of bed, pull my uniform on and quickly make the bed. The sheets I roughly haul up in one swift move, but the surface cover must be smooth without any creases. I run my hand over it several times and tuck in the corners.

The Colonel is in the kitchen cooking breakfast over the stove. She is in her dressing gown and still has curlers in her hair. Her face looks tired after another long night of duty, typing up the General's reports.

It is my duty to vacuum the camp in the morning. The vacuum cleaner is under the General and Colonel's bed and I have to time it so the General doesn't return to his barracks while I'm taking it out. He is in the washroom, so I duck into his barracks, pull out the cleaner and put it at the end of the hall, near the front door to do after breakfast.

I turn around and the General is coming down the hall from the washroom. I freeze and I know I must say, "Good morning, Dad," so with great difficulty I force my mouth around the words.

But the General is not impressed. "What the bloody hell is the vacuum doing at the end of the bloody hall?" He picks up the cleaner and throws it through the glass door and out onto the concrete porch. The glass gets picked up and we all continue as if nothing has happened.

Breakfast has been served by the Colonel in the mess. There is a plate with cubes of butter on it. The General has instigated food rations. As soon as I finish wiping the breakfast dishes I go out onto the porch and reassemble the vacuum cleaner and get on with the vacuuming.

The General wants me to do along every edge and every corner. I mustn't forget the red mat in front of the fireplace. It has a white fringe at either end and after vacuuming it I have to flick the white fringe so that none of the threads are caught underneath. When he isn't watching, I skim over some areas. Now I have to think about how I am going to get the vacuum cleaner back under the bed.

I enter my barracks. The General has carried out barracks inspection and my usual mess has gone. I open my wardrobe door. A jumble of schoolbooks, clothes and papers. Once again I have disobeyed the order, "all surfaces must be clean, clear or well organised." I look at the chaos in my wardrobe and start wading my way through it to gain some level of order. I finally get my schoolwork sorted and packed into my bag.

Next I must get the floor spotting duty done. I get the Chemico and a cloth out of the cupboard. After wetting the cloth, I get down on my hands and knees and crawl around the kitchen and mess floor, wiping off any marks I can see. I feel very vulnerable down on the floor and have to keep myself on guard, in case the General comes behind me and kicks me in the rear when I'm not looking.

The General rushes into the kitchen. He has preened himself to make his grand entrance into the world for the day. His toupee has been meticulously brushed. His false teeth have been soaked in Steradent overnight, vigorously brushed, and are now sparkling clean. His shoes are highly polished and his trousers have a perfect line down the front where the Colonel has steam pressed them.

The Colonel is finishing off kitchen duties. The General, about to dive out the door, says, "This is not good enough. You'll just have to get up earlier. I'm late again." And with that he is gone.

Now I must get to school.

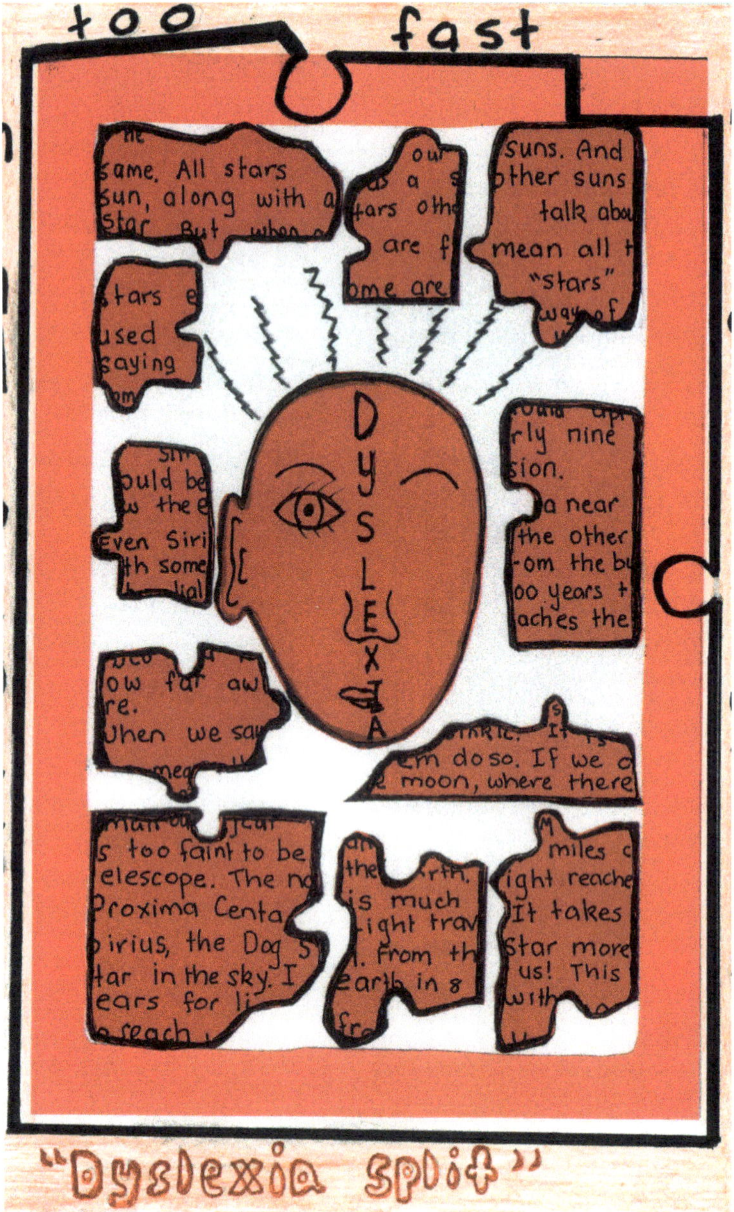
too fast
DYSLEXIA
"Dyslexia split"

School,
words firing
too fast too fast
head jammed
pressure
freeze.

Words mmoving
ju
m
ping
can't keep up
page fragmented.

Words tangled
talking muddled mudddle
disjointed
mind block.
Limbs uncoordinated
awkward
clumsy.
What's wrong, what's wrong?

In 1973, at age seventeen, a voice tells me, "If you sunbathe more and more, you will look and feel better." I stare in the mirror at my dry red face and attack it with my hands, frantically rubbing the itchy peeling areas.

My surface feels ugly and ruined
and my connection to the outside world
is shattered.
I stagger on blindly
with headaches behind my eyes.
I'm suffocating, and
there is nowhere to turn,
nowhere to escape.

Time blurs on and the end of 1976 has arrived:

The General is admitted as a day
patient
to the Mental Hospital.
He wants to climb
on the roof and jump off.
He tells me about the patients
in his ward and what he does there
during the day.

MENTAL HOSPITAL

One month later, I am in the Doctor's office. She says that
I must go into the Mental Hospital, Ward 10, otherwise
I will be committed.

I am taken over to the Ward 10 block. It is connected
by a long corridor and a door through to Ward 9—the
acute wards. I sit outside in the sun. It is late afternoon.

The sun penetrates and traps me. I feel terrified and alone, with nothing to grip onto, but I keep this down and sit frozen for a long time.

The bell goes and I am ushered into the dining room. There are buns for dinner tonight. I sit eating, but my mind is still racing and I quickly finish and go and sit in my allocated room. It is a tiny room, one small window, a bed, a wardrobe and a side table. I sit down on the bed. My stomach is aching and my whole body is taut. I try to keep pushing down the scream inside me, but I no longer can. I start screaming. The scream feels too powerful for my body.

LOCKED INSIDE

Evening moves into night.
A patient is banging
loudly on the wall while
I sit on my bed
trying to strangle myself
with my dressing gown cord.

Morning breaks.
I frantically dress and run
across to the bathroom area.
I look in the mirror.

Evil looks back at me,
the war in my head.
Eyes harrowed and wild –
racing fast in their sockets.
Skin yellow and red.
Hair dishevelled.

I run back out of the bathroom.
Can't tell them.
I mustn't tell them.
I must get to a phone.

Someone must save me from this.
I cannot save myself.
I run down the long corridor
through the door into Ward 9
and then down another long corridor.
The patients and staff are just
blurs out of the corner of my eye.

I get to the phone, but the
numbers in my mind are a
jumble. I try to remember
the Colonel's phone number
but the numbers are racing past me.
I dial but it doesn't come out right.
Patients waiting to use the phone
stand watching me.

The nurse is in training.
He is meant to protect me,
but he takes from me instead —
his lies are uniform blue,
masquerading as the truth.
He opens wide an untouched door,
then turns and walks away.

27 | Well-Come Grace

Someone is crying, "I want to go home,
    I want to go home," just like me.
Someone is receiving shock treatment
    behind a closed door.
Someone is walking straight and rigid
    and talking in a robot voice.

Someone is lying in bed. Her hands
    are moving in front of her face.
Someone is slitting her wrists
    and having them bandaged up again.
Someone is saying
    I'm just like her stepmother.

Someone is in a drugged sleep state.
    A nurse sits by her.
Someone is screaming as she is
    carried into the shower.
Someone is smashing a cup
    against the wall in the dining room.
    Pieces lie on the floor.
Someone is brushing her teeth, reciting,
    "Cleanliness is next to godliness,"
    over and over again.

Someone has run out of the ward
    and jumped in front of a train.
I watch her husband slowly
    walking away with her black bag.

The nurse says I'm to stay
    and get well here.

[Mental Hospital Medical Notes]

02.06.77: Packed her bags and strolled off at
about 1:30pm and never returned.

*I run out of the hospital without
my bag. The wind rushes
through my hair, images flash
past me, merging together. I
crawl over the fence to get to the
station, my hands are scratched
but I don't care.*

LIVING HELL

Back at camp the General is yelling
that he is going to get me committed.
He talks on the phone but
the Mental Hospital won't have me back.

Black doors are shutting
louder and louder.

My bed has become another prison.
When I lie in it, I burn and burn
and no sleep can be got there.
Once bed was my refuge,
but now it turns against me.

Nights are a living hell.
I get out of bed and then get into bed,
and then get out of bed again.
Morning comes, and
I have had no sleep.

The General has opened the curtains
this morning before going to work.
I must run, I must run around.
Pull the curtains shut. No light.
Not one speck of light must come in.
I must have total darkness.
When the light comes in it exposes me.
Lets me see evil.
I don't want to see devils,
I don't want to see anything,
shut the curtains, spin around,
shut, shut.

I've got to ring now.
I run down the hallway to the
telephone.
If I just book a ticket and go
and see my friend in Oregon,
then I'll be alright.
I ring up the airline and book a ticket.
The ticket is booked now
and I'll never go,
but the ticket is booked.

I start rocking.
I rock and rock and I rock.
I put one hand on my cheek
and I push it in between my teeth
and I start biting.
I bite and I bite and I bite and I rock.
And then I start on the other side
until there is blood.
My face swells but it doesn't hurt.
I'm numb.

After the beatings,

my weight drops
and my body is burning.

Night and day merge together.
I start to talk gibberish and
repeat words and sentences
over and over again.

I take food into my room
during the day and throw crumbs
and crusts down the side of the bed.
I throw tablets down there too.
Tablets are my enemy.
They try to control me
and take me over.

The General yells,
"You're going to get out.
You're going to a gym and
you're going to get fixed up."

The General takes me
on the train to the gym.
I look down at myself.
I'm wearing my old corduroy trousers
with the broken zip
and a safety pin keeping them up
and a red jumper that hangs loose.
My hair is all over the place.

We get to the gym.
The General goes inside
and talks to the man.
The man is smiling.
The General has told him things
about me that have made him smile.

The General says
from now on I am to go to the gym
EVERY DAY,
I'm not to stay in the barracks.
Early in the morning
I'm to go down the hill
and get to the gym,
no matter what day it is,
MONDAY, TUESDAY, WEDNESDAY,
THURSDAY, FRIDAY, SATURDAY,
all six days I'm to go to that gym.

The next day comes and
I have to attend the gym.
I go down the stairs,
slam the front door and pretend I've left.
Then I go into the garage
and crawl under the foundations
in the dirt and wait till everyone
has gone.

It is late afternoon
and the General is yelling again,
"I'm taking you
over to the Mental Hospital,
I'm not having this anymore,
you're going to be locked up
and put away."

I am made to get into the back seat
of a police car. A prisoner.

We meet with the Doctor in the office.
The General decides to take me back
to camp for another night.

The end of my life is here.
    Nowhere to go.
    Absolutely nowhere to go.
Morning comes. I crawl out
    from under the foundations
    and go into the hallway cupboard
and get out the General's amitriptyline
    and some other drugs.
In the kitchen,
    I pour a glass of water
    and gulp them down.
I turn and start walking down the hallway.
    I feel myself falling.

[Mental Hospital Medical Notes]

30.07.77: Admitted at noon from the Public Hospital where she has been taken after a small overdose. Distraught, demanding and crying often about how she should not be here. Says she does not want to stay. Dr feels that she must and it is hoped that it is not necessary to commit her. Given Largactil 50mgms at 1:30pm, which settled her a little.

I've lost a day. I've been unconscious for 24 hours. The Largactil makes me feel worse and more out of control and more terrified. I am screaming.

The nurse shuts the door of the room that I'm lying in. There is no handle on the inside.

31.07.77:   States that she is now aware that she needs support and is willing to remain in this ward as an informal patient. She is feeling more relaxed and confident in the ward situation and able to approach staff and talk over her problems.

Because the threat of the lock-up ward is like the shadow of death hanging over me, I state to staff I will remain in this ward as an informal patient. The ward situation is continuing to terrify me and because of my shock and lack of safety, I am unable to communicate my problems to the staff.

01.08.77:   Picking up physically and not quite so demanding on staff.

I can smell the stench of drugs from my body.

02.08.77:   Feeling anxious this afternoon, and unable to communicate the reason, if any.

Because I have bitten my gums I believe that both my gums and teeth have been irreversibly damaged and I can no longer eat.

14.08.77: Made to do her own washing today and activated. A little more spontaneity.

I cannot make any connections between myself and the clothes and the point of the task. I am stuck in a lift with the light off and will be there forever. So there is no point in getting washed or washing my clothes as there is nowhere to go — nowhere to be.

28.08.77: Despondent, wailing (dry-eyed) and listless. Using her old manipulative manoeuvres again.

I am beyond crying, wailing is the only way to express my despair.

31.08.77: Wailing and being immature and ridiculous. Ignored!

I continue to be in an extremely distraught state today.

01.11.77: Quietly gaining confidence.

It feels too dangerous to show my feelings anymore.

25.02.78: Everything fine. Discharged.

Each day I plot how I am going to kill myself.

CONSIDERING THERAPY

There's no hope in my life.
    There's no point in my life.
I plan to kill myself next week.
    Jump under the local train
like that patient in the Mental Hospital did.
    Yes, next Wednesday
that's the day I've planned.
    So, why am I here sitting in this chair
talking to this psychotherapist?
    I don't know.
Something beyond myself
    compelled me to come.

She is asking me questions,
asking me whether I am suicidal.
She affirms my world
and creates a tiny crack
in my darkness.

There is a space in her group on Friday.
If I come on Friday of next week
I can start group therapy.

I won't kill myself next Wednesday now.
I've got the group on Friday.
I'll wait till the following Wednesday.

I make an agreement
    with the therapist.
I will not kill myself
    between now and next Friday.

I lie on the mattress;
my legs and arms feel disconnected.
She sits on the mattress
    and talks to me.
She doesn't make me
sit up straight before I answer her.
She doesn't tell me
    to behave in a certain way
    or describe my behaviour
    through her world.
I feel her coming into my world
    and I start to let her.

My father has been diagnosed
    with a malignant melanoma.
He has two operations,
    but he is dying.

I spend time with him.
He tells me how
when he was in the war
he walked through a mine field
and his comrades were blown up
    around him.

He talks of a time
when in the front line,

face to face with a German,
he managed to shoot first.
I share this with the group.
My father is in hospital.
He turns to me,
his face open and vulnerable,
and says, "Give us a kiss,
Suzie."
He dies in the early hours
of the morning.

I trust the therapist now
to tell her how
I can only eat soft sloppy food
because I have damaged my teeth
from biting my gums.
She tells me this is not true
and sends me to the dentist.
My teeth are cleaned up
and I start to eat solids again.

I won't need a nose tube
or a throat tube after all.
I don't need to die now.

The therapist helps me understand
the voices in my head:
– The destructive ones
I leave in a cage.

With the therapist
I feel secure and warm,
relieving the coldness inside me.

The therapy is a long process,
but some light comes into my life.
I make new friends, start work.
And with the therapist
I have made the first strong
and real connection of my life.
Her voice anchors me.

Now in 1986 at age thirty, the light begins to fade. Deep trauma from the past is surfacing and I'm not ready to deal with it. I move away from the therapist and back into my inner world, trying to chase away the pain that is pushing in on me.

BOTTLING IT UP

These tablets should get me back to sleep.
Some wine from the fridge will help too.
I still can't sleep,
so I unscrew the bottle top
and gulp more tablets.

The pill bottle is empty now and
I ring another doctor to get more.
My face is going from numb to burning
and my teeth are clenched together.

My mother's Pastor comes to visit me.
He takes me out for drives;
he talks to me.

I cannot hear what he says,
so far away in my mind am I.
But I sense
his presence of goodness,
near at hand.

And so, the Pastor
comes and goes like a
sacred haze on my horizon.
Wanting to grasp
what he has to give,
but feeling –
> too contaminated;
> grotesque;
> guilty;
> trapped,
to be able to attain it.

Instead,
I walk away in shame.

Art Commentary – Shattered

This collage shows the movement into adult years where splits did not sustain me anymore, and are shown as broken. This meant I no longer had bases to function out of. I was at the end of myself in a shattered and tormented state. My true self is barred in with a broken heart. In this prison, I have not incorporated or developed adult thinking, as I was accustomed to operate from splits whose thought-patterns were fixed. The jigsaw has added two splits from collage #1: the green split on lower right is the *Benefit of Therapy Split*. There was trust and connection with my therapist but the validation and new information was only available to me within this split. The red and white split (second from bottom on left) is the *Psychiatric Patient Split*.

[Mental Hospital Medical Notes.]

```
20.08.86:  Admitted to ward at 3:15am. Stated
           that she took an overdose of tabs
           30 x 6mg Stelazene because she
           wanted to die. Had a grand mal
           seizure lasted 3 minutes, frothing
           at mouth, good recovery, was a lot
           more relaxed,communicative after
           this.
           > Observe for any more seizures.
           Observe also, a suicide risk.
```

The Pastor persists, and comes to visit me in the Mental
Hospital.

SHATTERED

A seemingly distant figure
    standing at the end of my bed;
that person of strength,
    here with me once more.
Again, I long to reach out,
    to connect,
but my wall of torment
    will not let him in.

Another Mental Hospital
    – down South;
 a long way from home.
    Too far now,
    for the Pastor to visit me.

I run into the day room.
The radio is already on
    and it's talking to me.
The songs are talking to me.
They're telling me how evil I am.
    Evil I am.

The staff have given me
   the potato peeling duty.
I can't help peel the potatoes.
   I can't even get dressed.
Evil is attacking me from the outside,
   and they want me to get dressed,
and they want me to peel the potatoes.

I ring the therapist,
   just to hear her voice.
A voice is telling me
   I'm so bad I will go to prison.
I'm already in prison — a prisoner of war.

Voices in my head
   are telling me I'm Hitler.
Images flashing — evil, destruction, death.
   My room has become
   a concentration camp,
where I am captor and captive.
Outside of it there is food,
   but I am starving;
   a bath but I reek;
   clean sheets but mine are dirty;
   people, but I am in
   solitary confinement.

Snakes crawling in my mind.
My father's snakes from his desert
   have become my snakes.
Eyes beading, tongues flicking.
   I sit and rock and rock.

ESCAPE

THEY think I should stay
      in the Mental Hospital.
THEY have examined my head,
      but I am leaving.
I stagger down the hall with my suitcase.
      My hair is brittle and falling out,
      my lips are split open,
      my clothes crumpled and shambolic.

A taxi driver is waiting at the entrance
      to take me to the airport.
He says, "It's good you are
      coming out of there."
As I sit in the back of the taxi,
      the driver turns and gently says,
"Have you examined your heart with God?"
      The first rays of dawn light
      cut through the dark.

At the airport desk I pick up
      my prearranged ticket.
There is a tap on my shoulder,
I turn around and see the taxi driver.
      He places a coin in my hand,
the change I'd left behind.
I feel as though I have received
      a spiritual gift.

DAWN HAS BROKEN.

HALF-WAY HOUSE

I arrive back in my hometown
and move into a half-way house;
buy daffodils and put them in a vase
on the large dining room table.

Without fully realizing it, God's
love, shown through the taxi driver,
has penetrated my heart.

Though still desperate,
this love compels me
back to the Pastor.
God has visited me,
and now I respond.
I pray with the Pastor;
repent of generational sin
and my sin reaction to it,
and receive deliverance
from spiritual oppression.

His loving, kind, warm demeanour,
leads me to unwrap the spiritual gift

I have received – a gift of love, hope
and inner peace.

And then before my eyes
a vision appears.
Jesus walks into the Pastor's office;
a large suitcase in his hand;
"FAILURES" - written on the outside.

He beckons me to place
all my failures inside the
now-opened bag.
Visually, one by one, I do this.
Then when finished, Jesus,
without a word,
shuts the case, turns and,
carrying the case,
walks out the door.

In this split second in time,
my deep, devastating failure
is taken off me forever more.

A friend paints my room —
    pink with maroon doors.
She makes a bed cover,
    puts up a bamboo blind,
places an antique chair by my bed
    and buys me a ceramic dove mobile
to hang in the corner.

 I purchase a second-hand oak desk
    on lay-by. It is delivered before
      I finish paying it off.
     They tell me someone
    completed the payment,
   but I never find out who.
My desk is special and I position it
    under the dove mobile.

I buy a mat for the centre of the room
    – it is brightly-coloured, warm and fluffy.
My room has become a haven.
    I sleep deeply for the first time
      in a very long time.

My hair grows back strong and thick
    and my lips heal.
I buy new clothes,
    put on weight
and mix with the people
    in the half-way house.
I can peel potatoes now,
    and cook once a week
    for seven people.
     I enjoy the smell and taste of
      food again and can hear
the birds singing outside the kitchen.

The Pastor visits me
    in the half-way house,
    and we sit;
    talk;
    pray.

I tell the Pastor
    how different it is now –
    released from the burden of guilt;
    nothing to be ashamed of anymore.

And I tell him how God
    has wrapped me in cotton wool,
    so soothed, protected, loved I feel.
And how, out of his mercy,
    he has laid his love in my heart,
    where no one else could reach,
and given me knowledge
    that I am special,
    that I do belong,
    that there is a purpose
            in my life.

FORGIVENESS

I also tell him that because of this love and forgiveness,
I am now able to fully utilize insights and bonding that
I received from the therapist during the past ten years.

The Pastor talks to me about the spiritual deliverance
I received when he was praying. How it was never loud
or spectacular, but how I would discern when the spirit
had departed from me, and then when it had left the
room.

He talked also of how Scott Peck's book, *People of the Lie,* rang true for me, when reading it after the deliverance. For it expressed so well, that my problems were more than psychological – they were also spiritual, more specifically evil, and that required a spiritual response.

> I know I will never forget
> how God has used,
> first, the taxi driver,
> and then the Pastor,
> to save my life from
> complete destruction.

I leave the halfway house and move into a flat. Over the next eight years I will study, begin a new career, marry and have a child. Throughout this time I keep in touch with the therapist but do not actively engage in therapy. It is hard to give up therapy at this stage, but I strongly know I am being called to start building a positive foundation made of rock instead of past sand.

God in his graciousness gives me a way to do this by revealing a visual image for me to hang onto. This image is of a continuous fence with a gate in the middle. Beside the gate is a cross. On one side of the fence is darkness and desert. On the other side of the fence is a beautiful river with lovely trees, flowers and a path alongside it. I feel God saying to me *"stay on this side of the fence Suzanne; walk on the path you can see and get strong."* So for eight years every time I experience a flashback or traumatic memory I visually push it back to the other darkened side of the fence. Through this process I learnt to have a strong dependence on God and thus less dependence on the therapist. In the near future it becomes apparent why this is all necessary, as the work ahead is going to be tough and I will be drawing deeply off God's sustaining strength to be able to work effectively with the therapist again.

It is 1996 and at age 40 I know it is the right time for the long journey back into the unresolved trauma sitting in the desert; the darkness is pushing hard on the gate now. I return to the therapist, where in my mind's eye at the beginning of each therapy session, I open the gate and allow some of the darkness to come through so I can work on it. At this time, by being connected to God, I am in charge of the darkness and at the end of each therapy session I visually close the gate until the next session. By doing this I'm able to keep functioning in the present: –

Art Commentary

Heart link shows how my inner self, represented by a healed heart, is now able to connect and communicate with my splits. The splits are still part of who I am but now I am in control of them rather than the other way round. I am now able to incorporate information and validation from *Benefit of Therapy* split into my inner self and then to filter this information out into the other splits.

Heart Link Collage 3

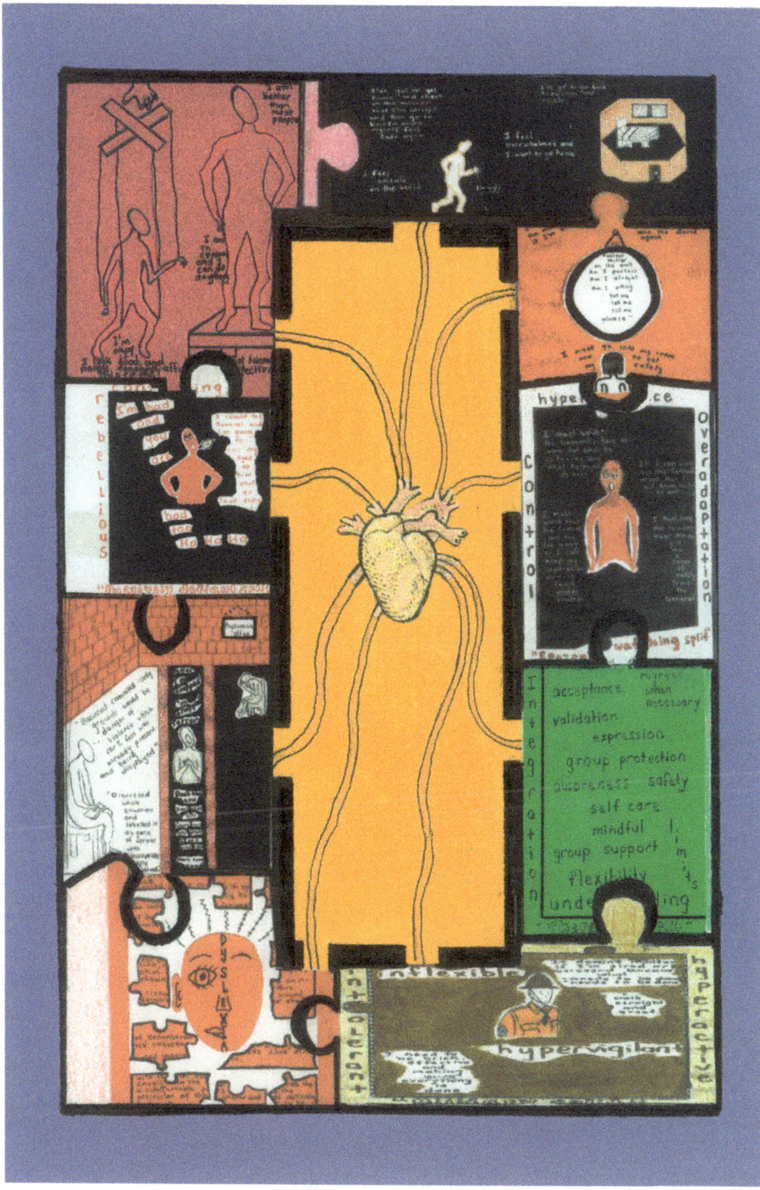

I take one segment at a time,
exploring frozen snapshots
with the therapist.
I write about the images
and get her to read them
back to me.
I express sorrow and anger
while she sits quietly with me.
I start to make links
and understand how
all the parts connect together.

Dyslexia is unmasked
and I learn ways to manage it.
I begin to paint.
I paint the snapshots.
I paint and paint
until the images are released.
I show each painting to the therapist.

I create positive spiritual healing images —
a picture of a dove
in the Mental Hospital
gives calmness and protection.
I write about this
and read it to the therapist.

I also paint these healing images
and put them alongside
the trauma paintings.
Heart opening,
parts connecting,
listening to the heart.

My mother comes to

talk with me and the therapist.
I tell my mother how painful
my trauma was and she explains
how it was for her.
We cry and hug each other.

I remember my father's words
as he was dying,
"Give us a kiss, Suzie."
Reaching out,
making his peace with me.
I take in his words and am at peace.
Now I reach back to him with love.

I revisit the closed Mental Hospital. I look down the long corridor of the Mental Hospital between Wards 10 and 9 where I used to run to the phone. Now it has died — it is only a shell — no staff, no patients.

I look out the windows to the left side of the hall. The courtyard is overgrown with a clothesline in the middle — bent and rusty. An old chair and an empty cardboard box sit abandoned and a red bucket lies empty on its side in the far corner. The wind is blowing up and I can hear doors rattling down in Ward 9.

Here is the smell I smelt 20 years ago, a combination of years of institutional cooking mixed with disinfectant and smoke.

I walk into the dining room. A notice on the door reads, "Please wear shoes in the dining room as the possibility of broken glass and china may cut your feet."

The kitchen looks dead and dirty. There is rubbish in the corner in a plastic bag. The cupboard doors are pulled open — an old aluminium pot lies on its side in a bottom shelf. The dusty sinks sit empty and streaks of fat line the ceiling.

I walk back into the corridor past the pool table room. There is a sign on the door, "Please keep door shut, to keep smoke in."

Further on, the cubicles are all lined up exactly as they had been 20 years ago. I know which was the one that I had slept in for nearly seven months. It feels the size of a shoebox.

I meet with the retired psychiatrist from the Mental Hospital. I tell her how it was for me back then and she tells me that she never thought it was my fault and that she never saw me as bad.

WELL-CONNECTED

I join an art studio
for people who have been in
the mental health system.

I create terrains for my trauma paintings;
the valley, the oasis, the desert.
I create a river of healing.

The validation and connection
I have experienced with the therapist
are now part of my being,
and I take them with me wherever I go.

The opposing forces of war
are reconciled,
the frozen snapshots
have become fluid
and my life, like the river,
flows before me.

In the desert
I have found the Well.

Art Commentary

Here the water represents the Well of God, which is the source for healing my heart. You can see my collage now moves into the shape of a tree. The tree's roots represent where I draw my strength from; God's power, grace and wisdom. This is filtered up through my heart and on into my splits; so transforming my mind and in turn my outward behaviours.

Poems in honour of
my birth family:

My Father

My father's life
typical of many of his generation –

A domineering father,
a submissive mother.

Second World War;
post-traumatic stress syndrome
being acted out, post war -
no understanding,
no treatment.
Stiff upper lip,
nil resolution or integration
of hideous memories.
I honour you my father.
Great courage,
perseverance,
discipline.

Would I have done as well
as you did, despite
mountainous odds?
I think I would not.
I have been given many hands
to hold on to,
but you had none,
other than my mother's.

So I salute you dear father –
an unsung hero,
who fought hard for his country
and for his sanity.

Rest in peace.
I love you.

My Mother

My mother –
you planted seeds of love
for God,
into my life.
Seeds that were watered
by your tears.

How you grieved for me
when I was ill -
and only now as a parent myself,
do I truly understand
the helpless pain
you must have felt
as I slipped away from life.

Yet dear mother,
you never gave up on me.
You saw me as a precious flower
that was still to open –
you saw beyond my illness
to who I was.
Thank you for your strength of character
and your incessant endurance.

I honour you now
for walking 'till death do us part'
with my father.
Yes, you walked the walk,
right to the end.
This has left a legacy of completeness.
A sense of wholeness,
integrity and love.

Rest in peace, I love you.

MY SIBLINGS

The four of us –
three sisters, one brother.

I came second in the line;
each separated from the other
by military structure and rigidity,
though under the same roof.

Despite this we loved each other
and it has never faded.
Like a waterfall that flows on and on,
so has this love flowed
through years of hardships and joys.

Each sibling
paving out a path despite early pain –
trying to pick up the pieces that our
parents were unable to deal with.

All striving to leave a legacy of hope -
to turn the generational corner
and steer ourselves and others
into the light.

Sometimes we live far
from each other,
and other times close;
but no matter where we are,
we carry each other
in our hearts.

I love you dear siblings.

PART TWO:

The Second Bite At The Olive

For it is by grace you have been saved, through faith – and this not from yourselves, it is the gift of God.

Ephesians 2:8-9

Yes, as we have seen, in my desert I found the Well – 'The Well of God'; that 'Fountain of Life'. There I was able to sit safe and secure, as his refreshing waters healed layers of trauma; like peeling back an onion until the last and hardest layer finally revealed itself…

RESTARTING MY STORY:

It is 2002 and I am now forty-six and a married parent. I feel at this stage I have completed therapy, having done the following:

» worked through my post-traumatic stress syndrome issues;

» integrated splits that developed because of these issues;

» made peace with God, myself, my mother and father …

» told the therapist my time in therapy has finished.

However, underneath all this I am trapped at my base. Trapped in what I will come to discover is Body Dysmorphic Disorder. I am trapped in my face. I believe I can never get out of this situation.

Having bitten the inner cheeks of my mouth in a psychotic state when I was twenty-one, I remain convinced that this has permanently damaged and deformed my face, and there is nothing I can do to change it.

Because of this conviction, I have decided that therapy has nothing more to offer me – that I have resolved everything that I was able to resolve and will now just have to live with any deformity and damage.

I can function now despite this, only because of my relationship with God and his love for me. He has so honoured me and I want to honour him in return. Also I have a sense of responsibility and accountability to my husband, daughter, siblings, my mother and late father and to all those who had helped me this far – the therapist, the Pastor, my church family and friends.

I have been blessed with so much and I know I must hold onto God's love and strength and endure on.

SCARY CHEEKS

I live each day in a base torment.
My face feels tight
and I live on the inside
of my mouth.
My mind visualizes
my inner cheeks
and I can see scars
where I have bitten them.

When I put my tongue
over the scars
it is terrifying.
It reminds me of how
I can never reverse
what has happened
and so never be able
to come to terms with it.

I wake up in the mornings
and my whole face
feels numb and round on the inside.
I feel like my being is tucked up inside it.
I tense my lips together.
My face feels like a ball.
    A ball of meat.
    I am distorted,
      disfigured,
        damaged.

I look in the mirror
to try and reassure myself
that my face is alright.
But it isn't.
My lips look fat
  and swollen.
    My face misshapen.

I move away from the mirror,
turning my back on it.
But I am compelled
to move back
to the mirror again.
    As if the mirror is a magnet,
      drawing me in.

Maybe this time
my face will be alright.
But nothing has changed.
    I am trapped in ugliness
      and revulsion.

> I try and put
> this to one side…
> I know that I will not suicide
> because of it any more.
> But…
>   this part is tormenting.

I carry on like this for several more years. I keep this world of torment internalized and do not talk to my husband or daughter about what is happening for me in my head.

I also carry this burden of torment in my work environment where I relate to colleagues whilst having words of deformity and damage chatting away inside of me.

I do my compulsive checking in the mirror in secret and keep drawing off God's mighty strength and the love of my husband, daughter, friends and extended family to keep me moving on.

BUT THEN

An awakening wells up in me… God has brought me so far and I start to think, surely he will not leave me with this bottom layer of torment – *there must be something I can do.*

RESEARCH

> I decide to find out about biting cheeks.
> Have other people done this too,
> or am I the only person
> in the world who has done this?

> I start to search the internet.

Has anyone else bitten their cheeks
to the degree I have?
My scars feel deep.
  I visualize holes,
    huge and red.

I remember the pain when I did it.
    I think with that amount of pain
and the number of times
    I had bitten my cheeks,
the holes with their now encased
    scar tissue, would almost reach
    through to my outer cheeks.

The internet shows me
information about people biting
the inner cheeks of their mouths.
I see that the scarring tissue
is called fibrous tissue and
it is hard and painless.

However, I still wonder about the
scarring tightening my face
    and around my lips.
I had also scraped inside
    my upper and lower lips.
I believe that I have thickened them –
    made them swollen and tight
        because of this action.

MAYBE

I begin to think maybe
there is something I can do.
Maybe I can get the scars
taken out.
Then every time
I feel inside my mouth,
I won't feel the scars and
so won't be triggered into
believing I am damaged and deformed.

This is the first time I have
felt any sense of control!
I feel excited, almost exhilarated at this
    thought.

I had talked to the therapist
    about biting my gums in the
    earlier stages of my journey,
 but had never disclosed that I believed
 that this action had in turn deformed my
    face.

So I now reconnect with her,
    and talk to her on the phone.
She says that cutting the scars out
    will not work–
if you take out one scar you will create
    another scar and the result
will probably be worse than
    what you already have.

I had not thought of this.
My sense of control disappears.

However, I am propelled forward
    again.
I tell the therapist
    that this is my
    last major trap.

I am surprised that I am back
re-connecting with the therapist,
for I had truly believed that I had gone
as far as I could with her.

However it feels like
the wind of the Holy Spirit
is moving me forward.
I cannot see where I am going
or understand why I am taking
the steps I am taking.
All I know is that God's power
is giving me a sense of urgency to take
the next step that is in front of me
even though the words of
deformity and damage
are screaming out
that there is no point to this.

I go to the dentist. I ask him if he could refer me to an oral specialist, to get his opinion of what damage has been done in my mouth. He agrees to send me to an oral surgeon.

The oral surgeon looks inside my mouth. He tells me that, yes, there is some scarring there. But this does not affect me cosmetically – that there is no abnormality in my appearance due to this scar tissue.

He goes on to say:

» that the scar inside my right cheek is just like a scar anywhere else on the body – it is nothing;

» that what I thought was scar tissue on the inside of my left cheek, is in fact normal anatomy;

» that the scar tissue inside the right cheek is just in the superficial layer of the mucosa;

» that there is no scarring in muscles;

» that if the scar was very deep then it would not be a fine line as it is in my mouth. It would be a lot wider and more proud.

LIGHT EXPLODES

It feels like light has exploded
into my brain.
I can hear the oral surgeon's words.
The words feel like
they are floating through air.
Like the thick fog
that was once there
has disappeared.
I had been to two doctors before about my
    mouth.
A long time ago,
at least seventeen years –
a General Practitioner and a Neurologist.
They both said there was
no permanent damage
done to my mouth,
apart from
a small amount of scarring.
But I could not hear them.

I WAS RIGHT – THEY WERE WRONG.

They did not understand
how it felt on the inside of my mouth.
They did not understand
how much torment and pain I was in.
Their words felt distant.
Way outside of my head.

But this time the oral surgeon's
words are centrally located
in my brain.
I can hear his words
alongside mine.

OBSESSION

I go back to see the therapist.
I am excited because I can hear the oral
    surgeon's words!

But I still need to take things slowly.
To rationalize the information I have
    received.
When I put my tongue
on the scar it
still reminds me
of damage and disfiguration.

The therapist and I start talking about
    OBSESSIVE COMPULSIVE DISORDER.

About how

I have a compulsion
to put my tongue on the scar
many times a day.

About how
I have the compulsion
to look in the mirror
many times a day.

We talk about how I
am going to make
an active effort
to not touch the scar
inside my mouth.
I share with the therapist
for the first time,
how I believe
people see me as
disfigured, deformed.
I share with her
how I believe my lips
look swollen;
my face
misshapen.

She tells me that my face looks normal.
She tells me that my lips look normal.
I am relieved to hear her words.
I trust the therapist
and I believe she
will always tell me
the truth.

I have not been able to
share my reality before, for fear that

she would confirm it.
And she hasn't confirmed it
and nor has the oral surgeon!

After my session with the therapist,
I go home and look in the mirror.
My face still looks misshapen.
My lips still look swollen.
And my face still feels tight
and deformed.

But the difference now
is that I have these new
words in my head.
I cannot apply them to what I see
in the mirror yet.

But...
I sense unravelling at a deep level
has begun.

I also share with my husband that I believed from biting my gums I had deformed my face. This is very hard to do, so long had I kept this secret from him.

He looks at me amazed and says that he has always seen me as a gentle, merciful person and beautiful both inside and out.

I cry with the release of having at last shared this with him, and I am aware this is an important step in coming out of the depths of secrecy and isolation.

LEAP OF TRUST

I have to take a step of faith.
These new words from the therapist,
the oral surgeon and my husband are in
my head,
 but in the mirror,
 my old reality reflects back at me.

I have to believe and accept these words
 despite what I see!

It is a giant leap of trust.
I have to move from
my reality and accept three
other peoples'.

What if I don't?
The consequence of not,
is now scarier than accepting
their realities.
If I don't, I will never
fully move forward.
I will remain in this
base torment forever.

God's small still voice is beckoning me
"... lean not on your own understanding"
     (Proverbs 3:5).

I know the word of God is true
and "… the truth will set you free"
    (John 8:32).
I have sought refuge in God's truth
many times before,
and only because of this
have I been able to journey thus far.

God's word commands me to move
to this new reality.
I have learnt that if I am obedient,
then fruit will come.

Again I anchor myself
to his word and, clinging
to the rock,
I reach forward,
embracing
the therapist's,
the oral surgeon's
and my husband's
 feedback.

The therapist and I have decided that in my next session
I will do some mirror work. She will help me process, as
I look into a hand mirror. This feels very threatening, but
I know I will do it.

However, for now I am
going to work at not
touching the scar
in my mouth
over and over and over.

I do this for many days,
but what happens
next is that I become scared
of touching it again.

I return to the therapist for another session. She
tells me not to focus too much on not touching the
scar, as that in itself becomes another obsession, to be
relaxed about the whole process.

MIRROR WORK

I take this onboard
and
try to be more
casual about
whether I
touch the scar
or not.

Over a period of months
something amazing
begins to happen.
Something, I believed
could never happen.

When I touch
the scar in my inner cheek,
instead of instantly being triggered

into feeling damaged, I am connected
to the oral surgeon's words
and to God's word...

"It is just like a scar anywhere else on
the body – it is nothing. The scar tissue
is just in the superficial layer of the
mucosa..."
AND
"Lean not on your own understanding".

With these words now attached to the
scar tissue, another wondrous event
occurs: when I look into the mirror,
my face no longer looks
disfigured – ugly – misshapen.
Instead I see the face of an attractive
middle-aged woman... me!

My cheeks do not look
fat and distorted,
and
my lips do not look
puffy and disfigured.

I cannot believe
what I see.
I am scared
to look away, in case
when I look back,
my old damaged face
has returned.

I purse my lips and they

do not feel tight.
This is proof
that I have not
damaged muscles and nerves
around my lips from
biting my inner cheek.
This is proof that the
oral surgeon was right.

My lips always felt tight, as if I couldn't move them
properly. But now, when I look in the mirror and see a
normal face, and then purse my lips - they feel relaxed.
In time, I come to realize, when I get tired or stressed
the familiar thoughts and sensations of damage and
deformity return.

Then,
when I look in the mirror,
my old disfigured face
looks back at me.

I know now,
this image is not real.
So, I wilfully attach my thoughts
on to the oral surgeon's words
and God's word again …
"It is nothing – it is just a scar like
anywhere else on your body"
AND
"Lean not on your own understanding".
The mirror clears - ugly duckling to
swan.

I want to find out more about Obsessive Compulsive Disorder. I never considered myself to be obsessive. This information from the therapist comes as a shock. But I see clearly that this is true. Before, I thought my compulsive actions were just a necessary part of coping with being disfigured and trapped in my face.

I venture to the internet again.
There is much
information on this topic,
but none of it quite fits me.
But then...
I come across a term
Body Dysmorphic Disorder.

I cannot believe my eyes.
I feel as if
I am reading about me!

I
read...

Body Dysmorphic Disorder (BDD), is also known as dysmorphophobia or the fear of having a deformity. It is a type of chronic mental illness in which a person can't stop thinking about a flaw with their appearance – a flaw either that is minor or that they imagine. But to them, their appearance seems so shameful and distressing that they don't want to be seen by anyone (Mayo Clinic Staff, *op.cit.,* 2008).

Some persons with BDD realize their concerns may be exaggerated, while others lack such insight. These delusional persons that lack insight are convinced their defect is real and believe that others view the defect as hideous or disgusting. Persons who have BDD spend many hours focusing on their physical features and engaging in repetitive and time-consuming behaviours resulting in decreased social, academic and occupational functioning. They tend to avoid social interaction, spend countless hours checking their features in reflective surfaces, discover ways to camouflage the perceived defect, constantly seek reassurance from others that their defect is indeed present or not so bad, and develop grooming behaviours to make the defect more presentable. Many are unable to stay in school, to maintain significant relationships or to keep steady jobs. Some may go as far as suicide (Slaughter & Sun, *op. cit.,* 1999).

People with BDD feel much shame about their perceived defects and associated behaviours. Secrecy is therefore common, complicating clinicians' ability to recognize and diagnose BDD. While symptom-free periods are rare, symptom intensity may ebb and flow. When one imagined defect is resolved, focus may change or switch to another body part. With fluctuations in symptom intensity and focal body part, BDD often goes undiagnosed for years. BDD often begins in adolescence. Sub-clinical BDD can start as young as age 12, and onset can be gradual or abrupt (Adams, Eberly, Wandler & Lee, *op.cit.,* 2007).

In many cases it appears that some event precipitates an initial elected focus on a specific body part (Thompson, *op. Cit.,* 2002).

I talk to the therapist at my next session
about Body Dysmorphic Disorder.
It is a relief to know that other people
have suffered this too.
It is a
RELIEF
to know that my
condition has a name.

Suddenly I realise Body Dysmorphia
underlay each unfolding breakdown;
deceiving me to follow a dead-end path.

So now I look back with God's light,
and see how it plundered
through my life
growing bigger and bigger
as the years went by ...

In 1967 I was twelve;
Body Dysmorphia began –

A hot summer's day
at the swimming pool.
My friend dived through my legs
and came up too soon.
Teeth crashed together.
Filling shattered,
mind snapped shut –
locked inside my mouth.

The dental nurse fixed the filling,
  but not the dark hole
  I had tipped into.
She said everything was fine
  with my teeth,
but I did not believe her –
my teeth were permanently damaged.

Pain, nausea, no focus, bite askew,
  not able to chew.
A peeler at school to peel my apple.
  A sharp knife to cut the apple
  into small pieces.
School kids who thought I was weird.
  But I was beyond caring.

Referred to my mother's dentist.
X-rays taken – showed no abnormalities.
The dentist said it was all psychological...
  BUT I KNEW DIFFERENTLY!!

After 12 months this attack subsided. Pain decreased
and I could eat apples again. What was left was residual
hypervigilance to clean my teeth and to keep them from
harm. Three years passed by and sweet sixteen had
arrived when another Body Dysmorphic attack gripped
me.

A blood vessel was on my face.

I looked in the mirror, over and over.
  It looked huge and ugly
  with a white outline.

I knew it was going to spread
   all over my face.
I knew people believed it
   looked ugly and gross.

REFRAMING MY PAST I

Summer returned and age
   seventeen rolled around.
If I suntanned my face, it would
   cover up the blood vessel.
If I suntanned my face, I would look better.
   I sunbathed my face,
   over and over and over.

My skin dried out.
   It was red and flaky.
I looked in the mirror –
   a hideous red face looked back.
The blood vessel was irrelevant now –
   false thinking, I decided.
But this time I thought I had
   permanently damaged my whole face.
The redness would never go away.
I was trapped, disfigured.

No one would want to look at me.
   No one would accept or love me.
I was a freak.....
   suicide washed through my mind.

The beast of BODY DYSMORPHIA was starting to devour me!

In time the redness in the mirror appeared to lessen and I thought if I never sunbathed my face again I would be alright. But this attack had left a sense of shock, and a hypervigilance for the redness to return.

At twenty-one I decided to go overseas. Nothing was working for me – I thought maybe this would help. I had an inoculation in preparation. My body reacted and my face went red from fever. I did not make a connection to this reaction – instead, Body Dysmorphia bit deep into me.

REFRAMING MY PAST II

When I looked into the mirror,
the beast glared back.
Red; Crazed; Demented.

I turned and ran.
But, I was ensnared.

Suicide was the only option...
I survived several attempts,
... and hospitalization
in a mental institution.

Again the redness in the mirror
appeared to clear.
Maybe my face wasn't permanently
disfigured – false thinking
I decided again.

BUT

I was much traumatised from this attack.
Agitation during this time had led
to biting my inner cheeks.
I could feel scars,

AND

I then decided I had deformed my mouth
and so misshapened my face,
and damaged my teeth again.

I tried to suppress these thoughts,
and hauled myself on.
But I felt –
Weak;
Vulnerable;
Frightened.

At thirty, I had been making worldly choices, taking
whatever I could, driven by a belief I would never be
loved – plus I was exhausted from illness – glandular
fever; mumps. In this burnt-out state, my suppressed
thoughts of disfigurement burst through, and completely
took over reality again.

HITTING BOTTOM

Lies pounded my brain;
biting my inner cheeks
at twenty-one had caused
permanent deformity of
my face and mouth.

When I looked in the mirror
my belief was reinforced –
for I had perceived a monstrous
face glaring out at me.
And I decided I would never
have marriage; children; career.
That this time I would never decide
these thoughts were false thinking.
I would be stuck here forever,
with nowhere to run.

Too ill; too shattered
to have fought back,
I instead succumbed

The Beast of Body Dysmorphia
had devoured me!!!

Only by God's grace did I survive – for he had come to me through that taxi driver, and planted his love deep inside. And even though at this stage I still believed the lies of Body Dysmorphia, God's forgiveness and mercy had enabled me to start facing layers of pain.

After this reflection, I feel blessed to have gained such insight into the destruction Body Dysmorphia had caused in my life. And I now realize, because Body Dysmorphia had stayed hidden for so long, trauma upon trauma had piled high – like a festering sore that wouldn't heal. But finally, I am unravelling the bottom layer.

MOTHER AND CHILD I

Now in my forty-eighth year, my
mother is diagnosed with
ulcerative colitis.
The doctors are trying to
prolong her life,
but she is dying.

Despite immense suffering she
exudes a spirit of courage
and endurance
and her faith in God
is solid and strong.
In her lucid moments
she tells us how much
she loves us and how proud
she is of us.
We tell her how much
we love her too.

She battles hard to stay with us
but each day she slips
further away. I watch her dying
and I feel a part of me
is dying also.

I feel deep sorrow with the loss of my mother. But, as the days move on I come to a new realization… through my mother's dying, new life has been offered to me. New life, because even at my age of forty-eight, the presence of my mother in my life had been like a shelter from the world. Now that she has died this shelter is no longer there.

> No one ahead of me now,
> to pat me on the back.
> No one to understand
> me the way she had.
> I need now to call
> on every bit of strength
> I have within me to run
> the rest of my race.

To do this, I know I must truly stand alone and fully use the key that has started to turn in the lock of Body Dysmorphia. I talk to the therapist again. I reflect on how my Body Dysmorphic attacks were always focussed around my face - my teeth; my skin; the blood vessel; the scar inside my cheek.

MOTHER AND CHILD II

> My delusional thoughts
> had a common thread:
> trapped; abnormal; ugly;
> different; disfigured; deformed;
> disconnected; isolated;
> no one could help
> and medication was pointless,
> as damage irreparable.

I never understood what
was underlying my delusions
and had no way
to prevent another attack.
Body Dysmorphia – master,
I – servant.

The attacks and delusions
started rolling into each other.
Lies, waiting to attach to content.
Terror and panic
underpinned delusional thinking.

Memories drift to my mother's words.
    H-bug in the maternity hospital,
    both of us ill.
Breast feeding so painful, so slow.
    Cracked nipples;
    breast abscesses;
        the use of a breast shield.
            Despite this,
        breast-fed for three months,
        but I never seemed full.

My early world of experience,
    a sensory world –
my mouth, my lips, my tongue.

A symbiotic relationship
with my mother.
Her pain, my pain.
Her anguish, my anguish.

TORTURED BABY-SELF

I talk to the therapist about sensations
in my mouth:-
Struggling to connect out;
A silenced scream;
Frozen.

I sketch these sensations and
realization comes –
the newborn baby part of me,
webbed in an endless
cycle of grief –
Struggling, screaming, frozen;
Struggling, screaming, frozen;
Struggling, screaming, frozen...

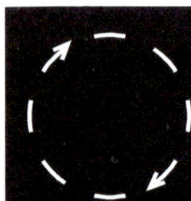

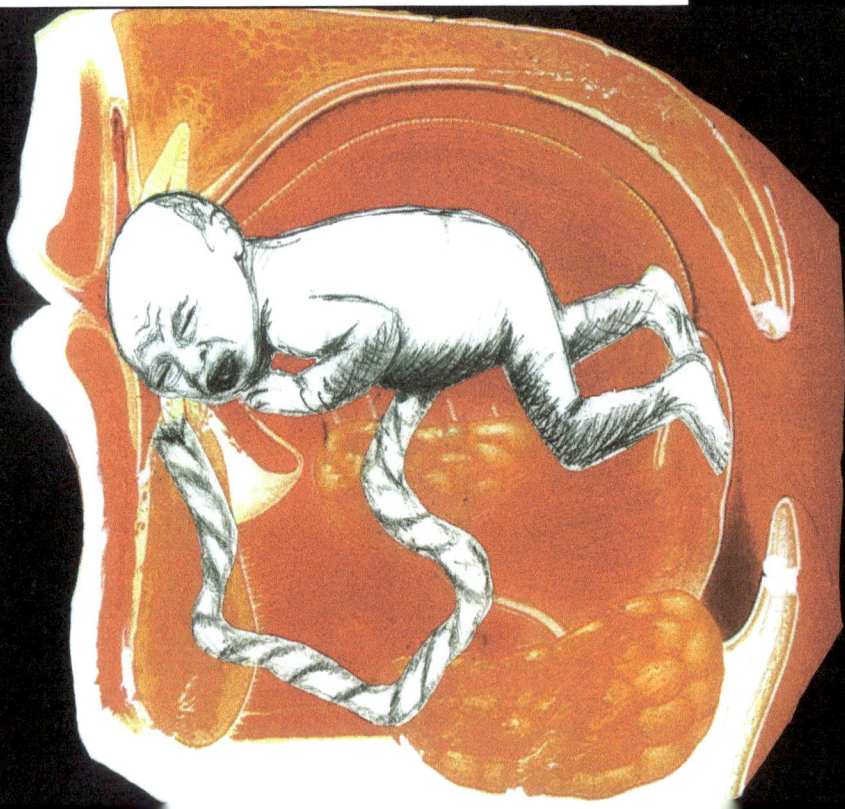

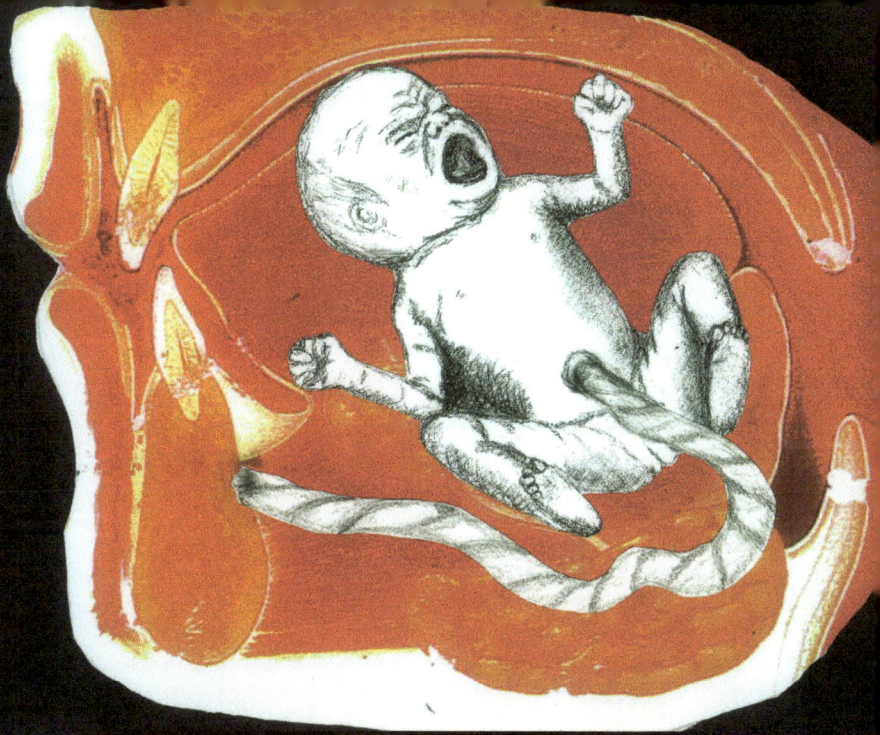

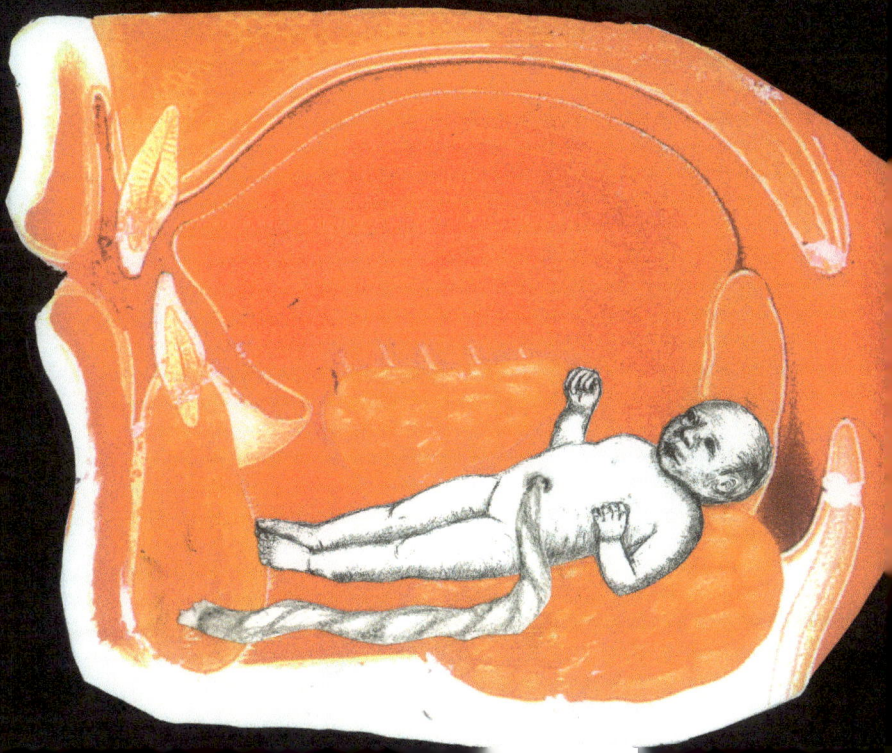

My newborn self – yearning
deep within.
Unresolved feelings; unfulfilled needs:
fixated at the oral stage of
development.
Stuck – internalized
in my mouth.

I spend hours looking at my sketched newborn self – meeting her face to face for the first time. I almost cannot bear the sadness I feel when looking at my sketches. For I had never understood till now, that the anguish and panic I had felt all of my life, actually belonged to the devastated newborn part of me.

So cleverly had Body Dysmorphia channelled these feelings; deceiving my adult-self that perceived deformity and damage was the reason for feeling such pain. I give the wordless world of my newborn self a voice…

Art and Words

Take a second look at the previous spread and look at it as a cycle: struggling – screaming – frozen; What do the colours tell you? Can you see that I've expressed a problem but not a solution…

In the next three pages, I add handwritten words out of black to the same set of three pictures. These are associations that arose in my mind meditating on the three states. For me, finding the words was a key route to healing: can we say:

naming= nailing?

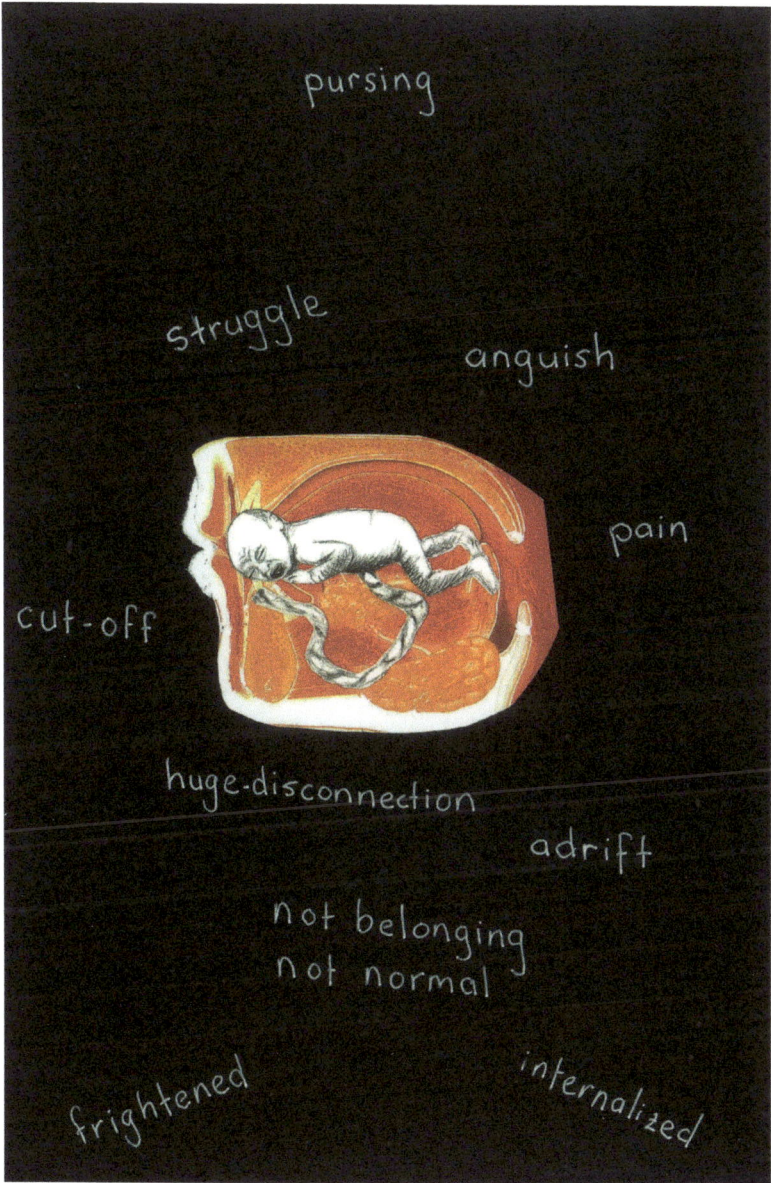

pursing

struggle

anguish

pain

cut-off

huge-disconnection

adrift

not belonging
not normal

frightened

internalized

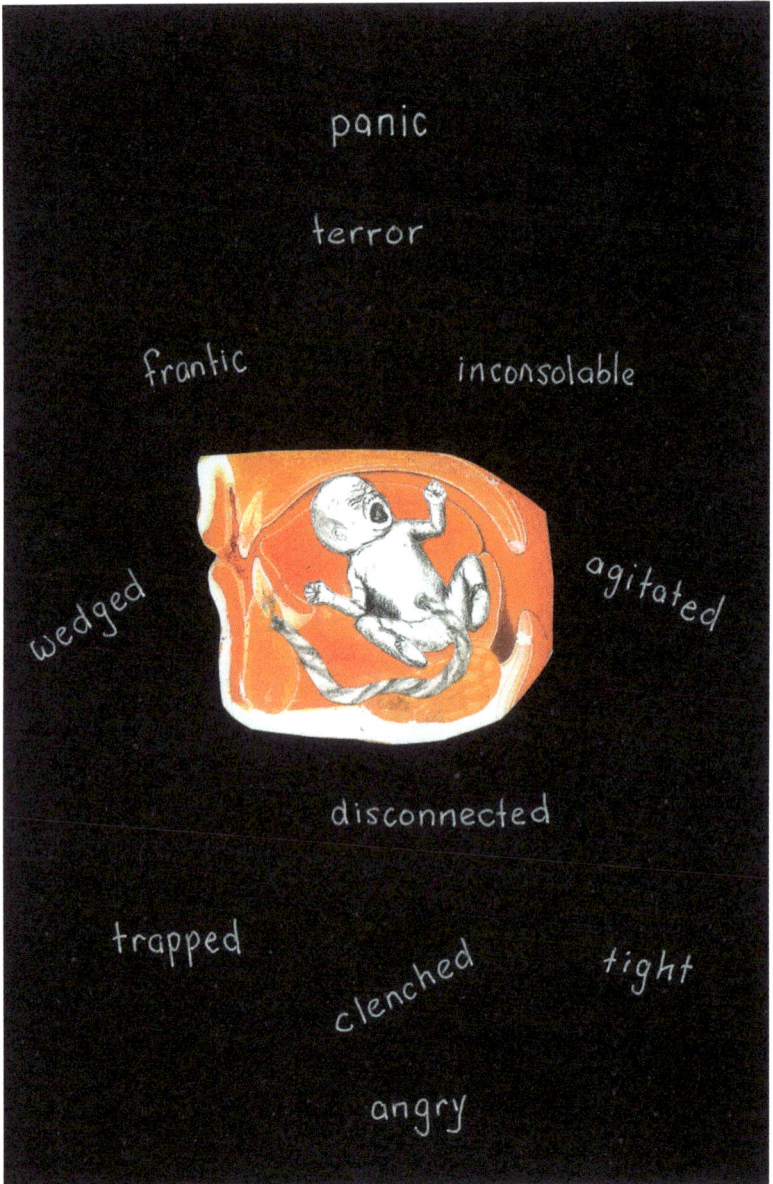

panic

terror

frantic   inconsolable

wedged   agitated

disconnected

trapped   tight

clenched

angry

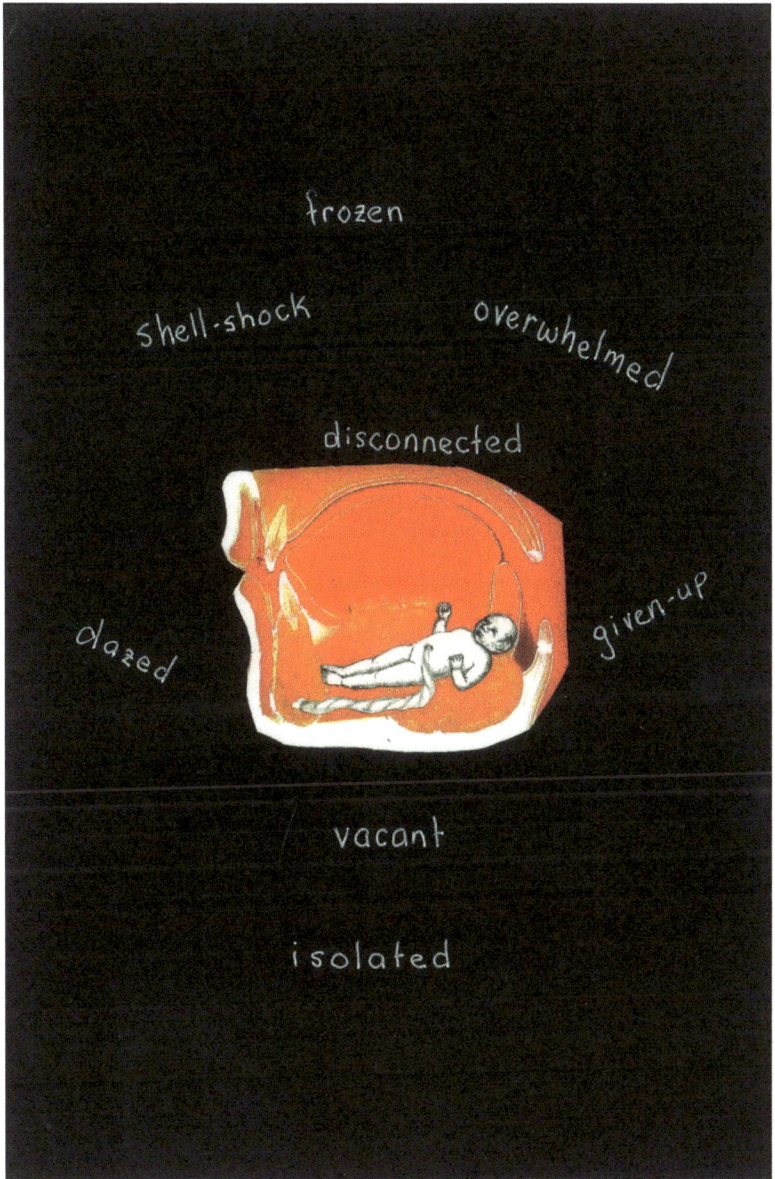

frozen

Shell-shock   overwhelmed

disconnected

glazed   given-up

vacant

isolated

NAMING = NAILING!

Pursing; struggling; anguished;
pained; cut-off; hugely-disconnected;
adrift; not belonging; not normal;
frightened; internalized...

Frantic; panicked; terrified;
inconsolable; wedged; agitated;
disconnected; trapped; clenched;
tight; angry...

Frozen; shell-shocked;
overwhelmed; disconnected;
dazed; given-up;
vacant; isolated.

**At last,
I have words to describe
my sensations and feelings.**

Revelation keeps flowing ...

Stuck in my newborn's
vault of unresolved grief – my adult-self.
Dancing like a puppet on a string.
The puppeteer,
my manic obsessive newborn self.

Grief masquerading as Body Dysmorphia -
a relentless circuit
that gave expression
to my newborn's sensate world.

My adult, trying to make sense
of this world.
But deluded -
succumbing to arrows of
Body Dysmorphic thought and action
that
blocked truth.
Believing my mouth deformed,
my face disfigured...

Trapped
Tormented
Stranded
Alone

I COULD NOT
    CONNECT TO THE OUTSIDE
        PRESENT MIRRORING PAST

Understanding comes...

Early feeding and attachment issues
drove Body Dysmorphia.

My base torment,
dispelled.

Transforming
by the renewal of my mind...

Whispered lies of Body Dysmorphia
have been taken captive.

Chains of fear
and condemnation
have given way to
freedom.

For the first time,
   my adult-self stands alone,
   separate from my
   newborn's grief –

Her struggle,
   no longer my adult's struggle.
Her scream,
   no longer my adult's scream.
Her frozenness,
   no longer my adult's frozenness.

My newborn's grief, of far ago,
    and my adult had tarried
    there so long.

BUT NOW...

Though not forgetting
what has been –
the past is
done with;
dealt to
and
settled,

I press forward -
discarding the old
and
clothing myself
with the
new.

"If anyone is in Christ,
he is a new creation;
the old has gone,
the new has come!"
                    (2 Corinthians 5:17)

BABY GRACE IS BORN

WELL-COME GRACE –
the new baby part of me.

You are:–
　Loved and protected;
　Well-fed and held;
　　Cherished and valued;
　　　Bathed in grace, blessings,
　　　　light, peace and calm.

　Yes, God in his love has transformed
　　my old baby-self into
　the healthy baby I was originally
　　designed to be.

Art Commentary

I should clear up a possible misconception, one that my editor made; the picture opposite and the next one over the page are not my daughter, and this is not about motherhood! I am going back to my early developmental experiences, which have been transformed through God's grace.

In the baby Grace painting on the opposite page, the hands and arms represent the adult part of me. Here I am embracing my new, transformed baby-self, and as such symbolising the movement away from my old tortured baby self.

grace

Grace the child within me now –
  eyes sparkling;
    connected;
      venturing;
        curious;
          resilient;
            free.

So now, when my old child's anxiety
      rears its head, I visualize my new
      child-self, Grace,
and her eyes steady the adult part of me.
 Her steadfast gaze grounds
      my adult and says:
that everything is in hand
      under our perfect father;
that I don't need to run
      to man anymore;
that man cannot save me;
that I am safe and sure with God.

Art Commentary

My new transformed child-self, Grace, is now the bubbly child that sits inside of me and from whom my adult-self draws inspiration. The painting Grace is holding symbolises the happiness and joy she brings into my adult life.

And in my mind's eye,
I see her smile and it delights me;
I can hear her laughter that lingers in
the air,
and she beckons my adult to smell the
roses;
to hear the birds sing;
to feel the soft gentle breeze; the
warmth of the sun;
and to feel her trust and faith in life.

I thank my heavenly father for my
new transformed child-self, Grace,
through her, the fruit of his Holy Spirit
flow.

*But the fruit of the Spirit is love, joy, peace,
patience, kindness, goodness, faithfulness,
gentleness and self-control*
(Galatians 5:22-23)

Now I praise God and reflect on how my life has changed
from inner stagnation to outward growth, as each fruit
of his Spirit flows through my new child-self, Grace; on
into my adult-self and out to the world around me....

THE FRUIT OF :−

» **LOVE:** from feeling unlovable to loving others.

» **JOY:** from feeling in torment to encouraging others.

» **PEACE:** from acting out of panic to calming others by my presence.

» **PATIENCE:** from wondering how long till I get through my problems and can separate from the therapist, to believing that in God's hands there is perfect timing and that healing will come to pass.

» **KINDNESS:** from being caught in my internal world, to caring about other people and what is happening in their lives.

» **GOODNESS:** from running from myself, God and at times the therapist, to having the strength and courage to face my issues.

» **FAITHFULNESS:** from isolation and disobedience, to trusting in God's promise that he will never leave me nor forsake me.

» **GENTLENESS:** from being hard and non-caring on myself and others, to wanting God's best for everyone.

» **SELF-CONTROL:** from being controlled by Body Dysmorphic thoughts/actions; professionals in mental hospitals; self-medication; body chemistry going awry, to yielding to the Holy Spirit's discipline and direction.

As the writing of *Well-Come Grace* is coming to an end, the Holy Spirit brings me back to the divine exchange at the cross - of how through the shedding of Jesus Christ's blood I was able to repent all those years ago and receive salvation. Through this provision at the cross, my spirit, which was once disconnected from God reunited with him. I was set free from guilt by his grace and enabled to move on, knowing I was loved and accepted.

From here God in his mercy gave me a concrete way to heal, with my restored child-self, Grace as my foundation. He knew that my spiritual maturity was slow and tentative and it took time for my soul (emotions, mind, will) to be transformed more into his likeness.

I have also come to understand how important and special my body is to God; the temple of his Holy Spirit. This has enabled me to view my body through God's eyes rather than my own and to respect my body as being of great value.

The Holy Spirit reminds me further of another exchange that took place at the cross; the exchange of Jesus Christ being wounded that we might be healed.

I am prompted to reread 1 Peter 2:24 with a new understanding:–

> *He himself bore our sins in his body on the*
> *tree, so that we might die to sins and*
> *by his wounds you have been healed.*

And also Mathew 8:17:–

> *This was to fulfil what was spoken through
> the Prophet Isaiah:"He took up our infirmities
> and carried our diseases."*

This time, I gain insight that God's word is saying HAVE
BEEN HEALED and TOOK UP OUR INFIRMITIES and CARRIED OUR
DISEASES, which is in past tense. I joyfully comprehend
that God has made provision for me!

My eyes are yet further opened, as I recognize the
Holy Spirit has patiently been leading me all these years
into God's full provision at the cross - the perfect and
finished work of Jesus Christ.

Here, through the daily surrendering of my life, I
now know I can rest, assured in the knowledge that I
have left behind delusional thinking and entered instead
into the *true* reality.

A new journey has begun.

"I praise you, because I am fearfully and
wonderfully made."

[Psalm 139:14]

O Beloved Olive Tree

A personal allegory

Scattered around my text, you will have seen symbols of barbed wire and olives. The Parts I and II above told of my 'two bites at the olive'; this final section is not 'a third bite' but a poetic recapitulation of my story in a spirit of thankfulness for God's work of healing.

> The Olive Tree,
> a symbol of love;
> > hope; peace; new beginnings.
>
> And I meditate on times of Noah,
> when the earth had been in flood,
> and how the dove returned to him
> with a freshly picked olive leaf in its beak.
>
> Yes, a tree of old – a beloved tree to me.
> For its cycle mirrors my life journey,
> and I reflect now on this…

The tough young olive tree, able to withstand extreme dry conditions, representing my childhood, where times were harsh – early feeding and attachment difficulties; the family 'military' regime.

The olive tree's leathery, spindle-shaped, dark green leaves; silvery white on underside, reduce water loss. And long roots, silently, secretly, absorb water and minerals from the soil and channel it up to the surface.

I too was designed to grow in such a way, by my heavenly father's precious hand, despite becoming a vessel for past-generation pain. Yes, he knew my heritage story, and yet placed me where he desired, in order to fulfil his purpose.

And so, like the young olive tree, I quietly grew, not realising I was always in the shadow of my creator – being protected and loved and filled with his food, which enabled me to survive right through my early years.

> Slowly we had become older,
> the olive tree and I.
> And season had rolled into season,
> until the time came when the olive tree
> reached bearing age, and
> winter chilling was required.
> This was needed for it to enter a period of
> rest, and so initiate flower development
> – otherwise it would remain vegetative.
>
> I, too, walked the cold path of winter
> – mental institution,
> trauma,
> grief,
> despair.

And during this time I felt I stood still;
    no way forward; no hope;
    no light at the end of the tunnel.
But, like the olive tree which,
    in its stillness,
    was preparing for the next stage,
God's outworking of his purpose
    for my life was still
    mysteriously taking place.

The olive tree changes – small white flowers appear in groups under the previous year's leaves, and because the flowers are either male or female or a mixture of both, wind pollination is the way the fruit will set.

And like the olive tree, I too needed a wind to be able to start bearing fruit – yes, without my knowing, the wind of the Holy Spirit had hovered over me, for prayer warriors had been praying on my behalf. So I managed to get out of the mental institution, and to connect with the therapist, who helped me survive.

Soon after completion of the pollination process one olive fruit is born for every sixty flowers. Then it starts its six-month journey to maturity.

Now, like the olive tree, I had also borne some fruit in my life. The therapist hadn't judged me but reached out a trusting hand. And tentatively I had reached back, and felt the warmth in the grasp.

At last the fruit on the olive tree
is ready to be harvested.
So a long-toothed comb
strokes the foliage,
and the olives become loosened.

And my fruit too had been
ready for harvest - though only a few,
and small in size.
But this sliver of light that had come
into my life at this time was an
important part of my journey.

In order to release the oil, the harvested olives are washed, crushed and pressed. Like the olives from the olive tree, I also went through a stage of crushing.

Dark torment from the past, which I could not fully face, and which had haunted me for so long, pushed through to the surface again. I was taken to a place where there was nothing of me left…

Another mental institution; a state of brokenness; and then God came to me through the taxi driver and the Pastor – he used this crushing period as a way to start setting me free.

The olive tree is pruned, opening the tree to light and airflow. And so too, in my life, through the pruning process of therapy again, God's luminous light and forgiveness had reached into layers of pain. As the dead and diseased wood of the olive tree is burnt, so, with the help of the therapist and God's mercy and love, my

thoughts and behaviours which were leading to death,
were severed for evermore.

> Finally, the olive tree matures
> and so had I.
> But the fruit we bore were not
> at their optimum.
> Though the mature olive tree's
> > roots are vigorous,
> and mine went deep
> > into the Well of God,
> something more needed to be done
> > for us both to become
> > truly prolific.

> For this to happen,
> > the olive tree must be grafted,
> > as it needs the stimulus of fresh pollen.
> And I had to delve down
> > into a deep layer of torment,
> where, with God's revealing grace,
> > I turned back the key in the lock
> > > of Body Dysmorphia.

The olive tree is grafted by a process in which branches
from a good quality olive tree are surgically inserted
into the tissue of the mature, strong, root-stock olive
tree. This is a labour-intensive process, but it receives
its reward – for when the grafting union has healed, the
good quality olive tree branches and mature, strong,
root-stock olive tree are now a single entity.

I too went through a process so profound,
    where I ventured into the anguish
    of the newborn part of me.
Here God the grafter,
    in his faithfulness, transformed
    my old tormented baby-self
    into the healthy baby
    I was originally designed to be.
And because this was such
    an amazing blessing,
    I named this grafted-in part of me, Grace.

Although it has taken time
    for the wonderful fruit to come forth,
      beautiful,
        life giving,
          superior fruit has now covered
            the mature olive tree.

So too, by the outworking
    of the Holy Spirit
    through grace,
    the priceless fruit
    pass through me.
And the rich and pure oil within the olive
    fruit reflects the richness and purity
      of grace in my life.
The now magnificent olive tree
    is a home to small insects
    and nesting birds;
    a shade to the weary,
and through bearing fruit
    year after year
      gives food to the hungry.

I, too, have now been called in my life
to flow on God's goodness
to those who are tired and faint:
provide shelter for those
who carry heavy loads;
and to be one of his lights
in a darkened world.

Days move into weeks...
weeks into months...
months into years ...

and
the olive tree
like me
is growing old:
however, unless the olive tree
is uprooted,
it will never die.

So too, with the
'Enigma in my Mirror' –
if the roots of
Body Dysmorphia had not
been
understood;
uprooted,
by God's revealing grace,
the beast
in my mirror

would never
have
died.

Yet, though it no longer lives there,
another enigma has come
to take its place:
my reflected
now normal-looking face;
dream-like,
untouchable,
veiled,
disappearing when
I walk away.

But the '*true enigma*'
– God's word, my '*true mirror*' –
the revealer of my innermost being;
teaching, healing,
cleansing,
from inside out;
opening the door
to His hidden treasures,
and secrets
and truth.

For at present we are observing by means of a
mirror, in an enigma, yet then face to face.
[I Corinthians 13:12, Concordant Version;
For the 'decoder' metaphor below, I have
benefitted from the insights of Mr Pouliot,
see "Reference List" on page 121f.]

And like the old olive tree
now with a gnarled trunk:
architecture of twists and turns,
protuberances,
knots,
and who never gives up;
I too must keep delving
deep into God's word:
journeying with the enigma decoder
– His Holy Spirit –
on an adventure of obedience,
to discover who I really am
in Him.

For I am beginning to see me,
how God sees me,
rather than the reflection of illusion
on the wall,
and when I finally finish my race,
God's revelation will be complete.

After 200 years the olive tree's trunk will disappear and
its root system will push out new shoots and produce
another tree. And like the olive tree, new shoots of
God's revelation have already appeared in my life, and
in my mind's eye I visualize my renewed child-self,
Grace, curled up, resting by the shoots of the new olive
tree – symbolising God's legacy of love and hope, to be
passed on through generations to come.

Epilogue:
Recommendations

I hope in the telling of *Well-Come Grace* that you as a reader will be able to short-cut your diagnosis and healing journey. It has taken me a long time to complete mine, in part because BDD is a relatively recent category, only recognized by the Amercian Psychiatric Association since 1987. However our Lord is kind and gracious and he illuminated my path as I tread.

If through the reading of *Well-Come Grace* you have come to a place where you see symptoms of Body Dysmorphia in yourself, I strongly advise you to contact a professional with experience in this area in order to clarify whether this a valid diagnosis for you.

Once diagnosed, I recommend you seek out holistic Christian counselling (spirit, soul and body). This outreach is important because, as you can see from my writing, Body Dysmorphia can become a chronic and long drawn out illness if it is not unmasked early in the therapeutic journey.

Acknowledgments

Thank you to my psychotherapist who walked with me, right to my therapeutic journey's end.

My gratitude also to the late Dr Ian Campbell for his care and support through many years.

To my dear friend Vanessa, thank you for the great times we have shared together.

Thank you also to my friend Judy whose love and friendship I will always cherish. To Bonnie for our long hours of sharing and encouragement in writing this book. To Nita for your inspiring words and to Gail who was always there for me.

My heartfelt gratitude goes to Pastor Rodney Duncan, for his unceasing prayers and spiritual care through the early stages of my journey.

Thank you also to Pastor Gary Colville, for unwavering care, and support over the past decade.

To my siblings, thank you for the bond we have between us. To my husband and daughter, thank you for your love.

Reference List

Adams, E., Eberly, M.C., Wandler, K. & Lee, Y. 2007 *Body Dysmorphic Disorder and Eating Disorders.*

CONCORDANT VERSION :1 Corinthians 13:12 was taken from *The Concordant Literal New Testament,* published by Concordant Publishing Concern.

Mayo Clinic Staff 2008, *Body Dysmorphic Disorder,* www.mayoclinic.com, accessed 7 January 2009

Phillips, K. A., 2005, *Understanding and Treating Body Dysmorphic Disorder:* Revised and Expanded Edition. Oxford University Press Inc.

Pouliot , Stuart H., God & His Word – An Enigma. "We See in a Mirror Dimly". In *The Upward Call,* February 11, 2012. http://www.kingdomandglory.com/ Accessed 5 September 2013.

Slaughter, J.R. & Sun, A.M. 1999, *In Pursuit of Perfection: A Primary Care Physician's Guide to Body Dysmorphic Disorder.* American Family Physician, October 15, 1999 http://www.aafp.org Accessed 5 January 2004

The Remuda Review 6(3), http://www.remudaranch.com, Accessed 1 February 2009

Thompson, J.K. 2002, *Body Image and Body Dysmorphic Disorder*. Interview with Dr J. Kevin Thompson, http://www.athealth.com Accessed 5 January 2004.

Bibliography

Blank, W. , *Grafting*, in The Church of God Daily Bible Study; www.keyway.ca, accessed 30 December 2004

Dankenbring, W. F., *Mystery of the Olive Tree*. www.triumphpro.com, accessed 14 September 2009

Hagin, Kenneth E., *Seven Things You Should Know About Divine Healing* Kenneth Hagin Ministries, Inc., Tulsa, OK.

Peck, M.Scott, *People of the Lie: The Hope For Healing Human Evil,* Simon & Schuster, NY, 1983

Renowden, G. , *The Olive Book* Canterbury University Press, Christchurch, NZ, 1999

Richison, Dr Grant C., 2003, 1 Corinthians 13:12, in *Verse by Verse Commentary,* January 4, 2003. http://versebyversecommentary.com/ Accessed 6 Sept.2013.

The Holy Land. 1997, *The Olive Tree.* www.christusrex.org, accessed 30 December 2004

Wood, Ed, 1998, *God's Word as a Mirror,* Sermon shared by Ed Wood, October, 1998; http://www.sermoncentral.com Accessed 6 September 2013.